Profitable Trades

Shaykh Abdur Razzaaq bin Abdul Muhsin al-Badr

© Maktabatulirshad Publications, USA

ISBN: 978-1-9432-7802-2

First Edition: Ramadhaan 1436 A.H./July 2015 C.E.

Cover Design: Abdur Rahman Williams

Translation by Abdullah Ali Somali
Revision by Rasheed Ibn Estes Barbee

Editing by Maktabatulirshad staff

Typesetting & Formatting by Aboo Sulaymaan Muhammad AbdulAzim bin Joshua Baker

Printing: Ohio Printing

Subject: Admonition

Website: www.maktabatulirshad.com
E-mail: info@maktabatulirshad.com

مكتبة الإرشاد
Maktabatul-Irshad
PUBLICATIONS

فهرس

Table of Contents

BRIEF BIOGRAPHY OF THE AUTHOR

His name: Shaykh 'Abdur-Razzaaq Bin 'Abdul-Muhsin Al-'Abbad Al-Badr.

He is the son of Al-'Allamah Muhaddith of Medina Shaykh 'Abdul-Muhsin Al-'Abbad Al-Badr.

Birth: He was born on the 22nd day of Dhul-Qaddah in the year 1382 AH in az-Zal'fi, Kingdom of Saudi Arabia. He currently resides in Al-Medina Al-Munawwarah.

Current Occupation: He is a member of the teaching staff at the Islamic University, in Al-Medina.

Scholastic certifications: Doctorate in Aqeedah.

The Shaykh has authored books, researches, as well as numerous explanations in different sciences. Among them:

1. Fiqh of Supplications & Ad-Dhkaar.

2. Hajj & refinement of Souls,

[4]

3. Explanation of the book "Exemplary Principles" By Shaykh Uthaymeen (May Allah have mercy upon him).

4. Explanation of the book "the principles of Names & Attributes" authored by Shaykh-ul-Islam Ibnul-Qayyim (May Allah have mercy upon him).

5. Explanation of the book "Good Words" authored by Shaykh-ul-Islam Ibn Qayyim (May Allah have mercy upon him).

6. Explanation of the book "Aqeedah Tahaawiyyah".

7. Explanation of the book "Fusuul: Biography of the Messenger) By Ibn Katheer (May Allah have mercy upon him).

8. He has a full explanation of the book "Aadaab-ul-Muf'rad" authored by Imam Bukhari (May Allah have mercy upon him).

From the most distinguished scholars whom he has taken knowledge and acquired knowledge from are:

1. His father Al-'Allamah Shaykh 'Abdul-Muhsin Al-Badr — may Allah preserve him.

2. Al-'Allamah Shaykh Ibn Baaz—may Allah have mercy upon him.

3. Al-'Allamah Shaykh Muhammad Bin Saleh Al-'Uthaymeen—may Allah have mercy upon him.

4. Shaykh Ali Nasir Faqeehi—may Allah preserve him.

ARABIC SYMBOL TABLE

Arabic Symbols & their meanings

رَضِىَٱللَّهُعَنْهُ	May Allaah be pleased with him (i.e. a male companion of the Prophet Muhammad)
سُبْحَانَهُوَتَعَالَى	Glorified & Exalted is Allaah
عَزَّوَجَلَّ	(Allaah) the Mighty & Sublime
تَبَارَكَوَتَعَالَى	(Allaah) the Blessed & Exalted
جَلَّوَعَلَا	(Allaah) the Sublime & Exalted
عَلَيْهِٱلصَّلَاةُوَٱلسَّلَامُ	May Allaah send Blessings & Safety upon him (i.e. a Prophet or Messenger)
صَلَّىٱللَّهُعَلَيْهِوَعَلَىٰآلِهِوَسَلَّمَ	May Allaah send Blessings & Safety upon him and his family (i.e. Du'aa send mentioned the Prophet Muhammad)
رَحِمَهُٱللَّهُ	May Allaah have mercy upon him
رَضِىَٱللَّهُعَنْهُمْ	May Allaah be pleased with them (i.e. Du'aa made for the Companions of the Prophet Muhammad)
جَلَّجَلَالُهُ	(Allaah) His Majesty is Exalted
رَضِىَٱللَّهُعَنْهَا	May Allaah be pleased with her (i.e. a female companion of the Prophet Muhammad)

INTRODUCTION

All praise and thanks are due to Allaah, Lord of all that exists and I bear witness that there is no deity worthy of worship except Allaah, Who has no partners. And I bear witness that Muhammad is His slave and Messenger (ﷺ). As to what follows:

Indeed, business, trade, and the attainment of profit — as well as competing in it — are the ambitions of every man[1] and the desires of every servant. Every man in this Worldly life is a seller, buyer and merchant, setting out and either selling his (self) — and thus liberating it — or leading it to destruction. However, many people are heedless of the existing competition and pursuit in the attainment of the profitable trade whose benefit for the servant remains in his Worldly life and Hereafter. In this treatise, *Al-Mataajir Ar-*

---

[1] **Translator's note**: the word 'man' and the masculine pronoun, whenever mentioned in this book, include both men and women and are used for the sake of brevity.

Raabihah (The Profitable Trades), is some words about this trade— trade of the Hereafter with righteous good deeds. So, prayer is a trade, fasting is a trade and charity is a trade. Every righteous act that draws the slave nearer to Allaah is from these profitable trades. Just as there is profit and loss in the worldly trade, so is the case with this trade. Therefore, whoever believes (i.e., has faith in the Oneness of Allaah) and performs righteous deeds, will have a tremendous reward. And whoever turns away from *Eemaan* (faith) and righteous deeds will be in manifest loss.

THE STATUS OF RIGHTEOUS ACTION
AND ITS HIGH RANK

There are over eighty verses in the Noble Quraan mentioning righteous actions: Seventy-three of which are linked with *Eemaan* (faith in the Oneness of Allaah). This great number mentioning righteous actions is coupled with *Eemaan*, resulting in the mentioning of the reward and recompense for successfully attaining Allaah's (عَزَّوَجَلَّ) forgiveness and satisfaction, happiness in this Worldly life and the Hereafter, as well as a blissful living, attainment of forgiveness, mercy and other than that from the different types of fruits and positive effects attained by the good-doing believers: all of which serve as clear proofs for the status and high station of righteous deeds.

And the believer's zeal for performing righteous acts increases, because whenever the Muslim considers these benefits, fruits and positive effects, his diligence, as a result, will increas and his desire will grow. However, if he is heedless of them, he will weaken and become preoccupied with insignificant matters and worthless things. Thus, if he continues upon that until the end of his life, he will regret when regret will be of no benefit.

These verses that link *Eemaan* and righteous deeds prove that the two are inseparable and that righteous action is a condition for *Eemaan* just as *Eemaan* is a prerequisite for righteous action as in His statement (جَلَّجَلَالُهُ):

﴿ فَمَن يَعْمَلْ مِنَ ٱلصَّٰلِحَٰتِ وَهُوَ مُؤْمِنٌ فَلَا كُفْرَانَ لِسَعْيِهِۦ ﴾

"So whoever does righteous good deeds while he is a believer (in the Oneness of Allaah Islaamic Monotheism), his efforts will not be rejected." [*Soorah Al-Anbiyaa* 21:94]

His statement (سُبْحَانَهُوَتَعَالَى):

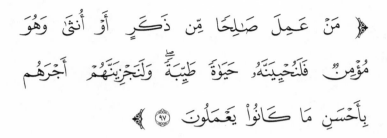

"Whoever works righteousness, whether male or female, while he (or she) is a true believer (of Islaamic Monotheism) verily, to him We will give a good life (in this world with respect, contentment and lawful provision), and We shall pay them certainly a reward in proportion to the best of what they used to do (i.e. Paradise in the Hereafter). "[*Soorah an-Nahl* 16:97]

His statement (عَزَّوَجَلَّ):

﴿ وَمَنْ أَرَادَ ٱلْأَخِرَةَ وَسَعَىٰ لَهَا سَعْيَهَا وَهُوَ مُؤْمِنٌ فَأُوْلَٰٓئِكَ كَانَ سَعْيُهُم مَّشْكُورًا ۝ ﴾

"And whoever desires the Hereafter and strives for it, with the necessary effort due for it (i.e. do righteous deeds of Allaah's

Obedience) while he is a believer (in the Oneness of Allaah— Islaamic Monotheism), then such are the ones whose striving shall be appreciated, (thanked and rewarded by Allaah)." [*Soorah Al-Israa* 17:19]

Similarly, the performance of righteous deeds is a condition for *Eemaan*:

$$﴾ وَمَن يَأْتِهِۦ مُؤْمِنًا قَدْ عَمِلَ ٱلصَّٰلِحَٰتِ فَأُوْلَٰٓئِكَ لَهُمُ ٱلدَّرَجَٰتُ ٱلْعُلَىٰ ۝ ﴿$$

"But, whoever comes to Him (Allaah) as a believer (in the Oneness of Allaah), and has done righteous good deeds, for such are the high ranks (in the Hereafter)." [*Soorah Taa-Haa* 20:75]

There are many verses that indicate this:

$$﴾ إِنَّ ٱلَّذِينَ ءَامَنُواْ وَعَمِلُواْ ٱلصَّٰلِحَٰتِ ﴿$$

"Truly those who believe, and do deeds of righteousness..." [*Soorah al-Baqarah* 2:277]

[13]

﴿ إِلَّا ٱلَّذِينَ ءَامَنُوا۟ وَعَمِلُوا۟ ٱلصَّٰلِحَٰتِ ﴾

"Except those who believe (in the Oneness of
Allaah — Islaamic Monotheism), and do
righteous deeds."

﴿ وَٱلَّذِينَ ءَامَنُوا۟ وَعَمِلُوا۟ ٱلصَّٰلِحَٰتِ ﴾

"And those who believe (in the Oneness of
Allaah (سُبْحَانَهُۥوَتَعَالَىٰ) - Islaamic Monotheism) and
do righteous good deeds..."

If a servant has righteous deeds without a truthful
creed in his heart and a correct *Eemaan*, his deeds will
not benefit him. Allaah (عَزَّوَجَلَّ) said:

﴿ وَمَن يَكْفُرْ بِٱلْإِيمَٰنِ فَقَدْ حَبِطَ عَمَلُهُۥ وَهُوَ فِى

ٱلْأَخِرَةِ مِنَ ٱلْخَٰسِرِينَ ۝ ﴾

"And whosoever disbelieves in Faith [i.e. in
the Oneness of Allaah and in all the other

[14]

Articles of Faith, i.e. His (Allaah's), Angels, His Holy Books, His Messengers, the Day of Resurrection and al-Qadar (Divine Pre ordainments)], then fruitless is his work. And in the Hereafter he will be among the losers."
[*Soorah al-Maa'idah* 5:5]

Equally, if a person has *Eemaan* but does not perform any good deeds and has none to speak of, then he is not from the people of Islaam; because, the people of Islaam and *Eemaan* are those who have believed and performed righteous actions.

These two matters are inseparable: *Eemaan* and righteous actions, it is an acknowledgement that is contained by the hearts and gives fruit to actions that show through the limbs as he (the Messenger (صَلَّى ٱللَّهُ عَلَيْهِ وَسَلَّمَ)) said:

أَلَا وَ إِنَّ فِي الْجَسَدِ مُضْغَةً إِذَا صَلَحَتْ صَلَحَ الْجَسَدُ كُلُّهُ ، وَ إِذَا فَسَدَتْ فَسَدَ الْجَسَدُ كُلُّهُ ، أَلَا وَ هِيَ الْقَلْبُ

"Certainly, there is a morsel of flesh in the body. If it is sound and upright, then the entire

[15]

body will be sound and upright. So if it is rotten, then the entire body will be rotten. Certainly, it is the heart." [2]

---

[2] Collected by *al-Bukhaaree* (52), *Muslim* (1599) from the Hadeeth of an-Nu'maan Ibn Basheer (رَضِيَ اللهُ عَنْهُ)

THE FRUIT AND EFFECTS OF RIGHTEOUS DEEDS

The fruits and effects of righteous deeds upon the slave in his Worldly life and Hereafter are numerous in number. A person must know that this Worldly life and what it contains from the delights, varying types of benefits and offspring, as well as what it contains from trades: none of this will accompany a person once he leaves this life and is entered into the grave, nothing will accompany him except his actions—righteous or evil. It has been reported by a Hadeeth in the *Saheehayn* (*al-Bukhaaree and Muslim*) from the Hadeeth of Anas (رَضِيَاللَّهُعَنْهُ) who said that the Messenger of Allaah (صَلَّىاللَّهُعَلَيْهِوَسَلَّمَ) said:

يَتْبَعُ الْمَيِّتَ ثَلَاثَةٌ ، فَـيَرْجِعُ اثْنَانِ وَ يَبْقَى مَعَهُ وَاحِدٌ : يَتْبَعُهُ أَهْلُهُ وَ مَالُهُ وَ عَمَلُهُ ، فَيَرْجِعُ أَهْلُهُ وَ مَالُهُ وَ يَبْقَى عَمَلُهُ .

> "Three will follow the deceased, two will
> return and one will remain with him: his
> family, wealth and deeds will follow him, his
> family and wealth will return and his deeds
> will remain." [3]

"His deeds will remain," means, they will
accompany him to the grave. As for a person's child,
he will not enter the grave with him even if he loved
his father and concealed for him a deep,
compassionate love. Also, a person's wealth, no
matter how abundant and varying it is, will not enter
the grave with him. Thus, it has come in another
Hadeeth reported by al-Bayhaqee in *"Shu'ab Al-
Eemaan"* from the Hadeeth of Aboo Hurairah (رَضِيَاللهُعَنْهُ)
that the Prophet (صَلَّىاللهُعَلَيْهِوَسَلَّمَ) said:

مَثَلُ ابْنِ آدَمَ وَ مَالِهِ وَ عَمَلِهِ مَثَلُ رَجُلٍ لَهُ

ثَلَاثَةُ أَخِلَّاءَ ، قَالَ لَهُ أَحَدُهُمْ : أَنَا مَعَكَ مَا دُمْتَ

حَيًّا ، فَإِذَا مُتُّ فَلَسْتَ مِنِّي وَ لَا أَنَا مِنْكَ ،

فَذَلِكَ مَالُهُ ، وَ قَالَ الْآخِرُ : أَنَا مَعَكَ ، فَإِذَا

---

[3] Collected by *al-Bukhaaree* (6514), *Muslim* (6960)

بَلَغْتَ إِلَى قَبْرِكَ فَلَسْتَ مِنِّي وَ لَسْتُ لَكَ ،
فَذَلِكَ وَلَدُهُ وَ قَالَ الْآخِرَ : أَنَا مَعَكَ حَيًّا وَ مَيِّتًا
، فَذَلِكَ عَمَلُهُ .

"The example of the son of Aadam and his wealth and deeds is like the example of a man who has three close friends. One of them says to him: 'I am with you as long as you live, but if you die, you are not from me and neither am I from you;' and that is his wealth. The other one says to him: 'I am with you, but when you reach your grave, you are not from me, and I am not for you;' and that is his son. The other one says to him: 'I am with you dead or alive;' and that is his deeds." [4]

On a similar note, Ibn al-Qayyim (رَحِمَهُٱللَّه) reports in *Rawdatul-Muhibbeen* that one of the wise men was asked: **"Which companion is most dutiful?"** He said: **"Righteous action."** So, the righteous action is a dutiful companion to a person. Look at this dutifulness in the darkest, severest and greatest of

---

[4] Collected by al-Bayhaqee in *Shu'ab al-Eemaan* (9993), authenticated by al-Albaanee in *as-Saheehah* (2481).

situations when an individual is entered into his
grave. In the *Musnad* of Imaam Ahmad on the
authority of al-Baraa' ibn 'Aazib (رَضِيَاللَّهَعَنْهُ) is a long
context that contains:

فَيَأْتِيهِ رَجُلٌ حَسَنُ الْوَجْهِ حَسَنُ الثِّيَابِ طَيِّبُ
الرِّيحِ فَيَقُولُ: ((أَبْشِرْ بِالَّذِي يَسُرُّكَ، هَذَا يَوْمُكَ
الَّذِي كُنْتَ تُوعَدُ)) فَيَقُولُ: ((مَنْ أَنْتَ ؟
فَوَجْهُكَ الْوَجْهُ يَجِيءُ بِالْخَيْرِ)) ، فَيَقُولُ: ((
أَنَا عَمَلُكَ الصَّالِحُ)) .

**"A man with a handsome face and clothes and
a pleasant fragrance will come to him and say:
'Receive the glad tidings that bring you joy,
this is your day that you were promised.' He
will say: Who are you? Your face is a face that
brings good. He says: 'I am your righteous
deeds.'"** [5]

---

[5] Collected by Ahmad (18534), authenticated by al-Albaanee in
Ahkaam al-Janaa'iz (pg. 159).

It has been reported in the *Saheeh* (*al-Bukhaaree*) that the Prophet (ﷺ) said:

إِذَا وُضِعَتِ الْجَنَازَةُ فَاحْتَمَلَهَا الرِّجَالُ عَلَى أَعْنَاقِهِمْ ، فَإِنْ كَانَتْ صَالِحَةً ، قَالَتْ : ((قَدِّمُونِي قَدِّمُونِي)) . وَ إِنْ كَانَتْ غَيْرَ صَالِحَةٍ قَالَتْ : ((يَا وَيْلَهَا أَيْنَ يَذْهَبُونَ بِهَا))

"When the deceased is ready (for its burial), the men lift it on their shoulders. If the deceased was a righteous person, he says: 'Take me ahead, take me ahead,' and if he was not a righteous one, he says: 'Woe to it (me)! Where are you taking it (me)?'" [6]

This, as well as other proofs, indicate the lofty status of righteous deeds and that whomever Allaah (سُبْحَانَهُوَتَعَالَى) gives *Tawfeeq* to (ability to be successful) in performing righteous deeds, they are the people of the profitable trade and the clear treasure; and other than them from the disbelievers or the neglectful will certainly regret when it will be of no avail to them.

---

[6] Collected by *al-Bukhaaree* (1380)

THE FRUIT AND EFFECTS OF RIGHTEOUS DEEDS

Therefore, the clever one from Allaah's servants is the one who holds his soul to account and works for what is after death; and the weak and crippled one is the one who allows his soul to freely follow its desires and has wishful thinking about Allaah (without putting in any effort). On a similar note, 'Alee Ibn Abee Taalib (رَضِيَاللَّهُعَنْهُ) said:

إِرْتَحَلَتِ الدُّنْيَا مُدَبِّرَةً ، وَارْتَحَلَتِ الْآخِرَةُ مُقْبِلَةً ، وَ لِكُلِّ وَاحِدَةٍ مِنْهُمَا بَنُونَ، فَكُونُوا مِنْ أَبْنَاءِ الْآخِرَةِ ، وَ لَا تَكُونُوا مِنْ أَبْنَاءِ الدُّنْيَا ، فَإِنَّ الْيَوْمَ عَمَلٌ وَ لَا حِسَابَ وَ غَداً حِسَابٌ وَ لَا عَمَلَ .

"The Worldly life has departed with its back turned, and the Hereafter has set out fast approaching, and each has children, so be from the children of the Hereafter and not from the children of the Worldly life. Indeed, today is for action and not accountability while

tomorrow (the Day of Judgement) is for accountability and not action." [7]

Allaah (سُبْحَانَهُوَتَعَالَى) said:

﴿ لِمِثْلِ هَذَا فَلْيَعْمَلِ ٱلْعَـٰمِلُونَ ۝ ﴾

"For the like of this let the workers work."
[*Soorah as-Saaffaat* 37:61]

Certainly, this is the profitable trade, not the one of the short-lived Worldly life which is surely a losing deal: its blessings are discontinuing, its good is short-lived, and its dweller will leave it after a short while. Therefore, let the servant be cautious from becoming a partaker in this losing deal. The scholars have drawn a parable for this as mentioned by Imaam ash-Shinqeedee (رَحِمَهُ ٱللَّهُ):

"They said: 'Verily, Allaah (جَلَّ وَعَلَا) has given every aged man a most-valuable asset of wealth; and the most valuable asset of this wealth is the jewels that cannot be measured or replaced by anything in the Worldly life–these are the most valuable assets of every person's wealth. By 'jewels,' we mean, the

---

[7] Collected by *al-Bukhaaree* as commentary in *Kitaab ar-Riqaaq* before the Hadeeth (6417).

[23]

hours and days of life; because, the most valuable asset of one's wealth and the most the precious and tremendous thing that he can be given is the days and hours of his life. So, just as Allaah has made this the most valuable asset of one's wealth, he likewise made it a brother to the Messenger in establishing the proof against a person when he said:

﴿ أَوَلَمْ نُعَمِّرْكُم مَّا يَتَذَكَّرُ فِيهِ مَن تَذَكَّرَ وَجَآءَكُمُ ٱلنَّذِيرُ ﴾

"Did We not give you lives long enough, so that whosoever would receive admonition, could receive it? And the warner came to you."
[*Soorah al-Faatir* 35:37]

So, if the aged man—whether he has been granted a long life or not as He (سُبْحَانَهُ وَتَعَالَى) says:

﴿ وَمَا يُعَمَّرُ مِن مُّعَمَّرٍ وَلَا يُنقَصُ مِنْ عُمُرِهِ إِلَّا فِي كِتَٰبٍ إِنَّ ذَٰلِكَ عَلَى ٱللَّهِ يَسِيرٌ ۝ ﴾

"And no aged man is granted a length of life, nor is a part cut off from his life (or another man's life), but is in a Book (Al-Lauh Al-Mahfûz)." [*Soorah al-Faadir* 35:11]

--if he is clever and tactful, he will know how to move and utilize the most valuable asset of wealth and benefit from it. He will direct it (i.e., the hours and days of his life) in that which is pleasing to Allaah; thus, guarding over the moments, days, nights, minutes and seconds as to not waste a single moment in other than obedience to Allaah. So, he looks at the times in which the commands of his Lord are fulfilled — like the times of the prayer, Hajj (legislated pilgrimage to Makkah) and other than that from the requested acts that are performed at certain times when they arise — and thus fulfils them for Allaah in the best manner. As for the times in which no functions or specific obligations from the Lord of all that exists are to be carried out, he restrains his evil, fears Allaah (جَلَّ وَعَلَا) and increases in fulfilling as much good as possible.

Therefore, if he does put this to work — the most valuable asset of his wealth — and engages this profitable trade with the Lord of all that exists, he will enjoy many pleasures: a kingdom that will never

[25]

cease, al-Huur al-'ayn (the beautiful damsels of Paradise), the Gardens of Paradise, the youthful servants, nearness to a pleased Lord (Allaah), and sight of the Noble Face of Allaah. And Allaah has called such a utilization of the most valuable asset of wealth in that which is pleasing to Him (جَلَّوَعَلَا) in the manner mentioned: **'Bay''** (selling), **'Shiraa'** (purchasing), **'Tijaarah'** (trade) and he also called it **'Qardh'** (loan); because, the individual capitalized on the most valuable asset of his wealth (i.e., the days of his life) in the best and most appropriate manner. Thus, He (سُبْحَانَهُوَتَعَالَى) said:

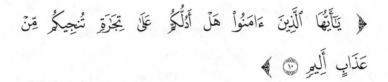

"O You who believe! Shall I guide you to a trade that will save you from a painful torment?" [*Soorah as-Saff* 61:10]

Allaah clearly states that this is trading with Him (جَلَّوَعَلَا), saying:

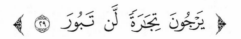

[26]

"...they hope for a (sure) trade gain that will never perish." [*Soorah al-Faatir* 35:29]

He (جَلَّوَعَلَا) also said:

$$ ﴿ ۞ إِنَّ ٱللَّهَ ٱشْتَرَىٰ مِنَ ٱلْمُؤْمِنِينَ أَنفُسَهُمْ وَأَمْوَٰلَهُم بِأَنَّ لَهُمُ ٱلْجَنَّةَ ﴾ $$

"Verily, Allaah has purchased of the believers their lives and their properties for (the price) that theirs shall be the Paradise."

Until His statement:

$$ ﴿ فَٱسْتَبْشِرُواْ بِبَيْعِكُمُ ٱلَّذِى بَايَعْتُم بِهِۦ ۚ وَذَٰلِكَ هُوَ ٱلْفَوْزُ ٱلْعَظِيمُ ۝ ﴾ $$

"Then rejoice in the bargain which you have concluded. That is the supreme success." [*Soorah at-Tawbah* 9:111]

He (جَلَّوَعَلَا) also said:

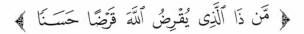

﴿ مَّن ذَا ٱلَّذِى يُقْرِضُ ٱللَّهَ قَرْضًا حَسَنًا ﴾

"Who is he that will lend to Allaah a goodly loan?" [*Soorah al-Baqarah* 2:245]

If the poor possessor of this most valuable asset of wealth is a foolish man who does not know the reality of things and who's interior has not been enlightened by the light of the Revelation (the Quraan); he will be unable to know its true worth, nor the estimation of these jewels that Allaah has given him. Consequently, he will put it to waste in 'he said' and 'it was said,' not gaining anything from it until his appointed time expires and is pulled into his grave empty-handed. And the Hereafter—O brothers—is an unbefitting abode for the broke and the poor, because there will be none to benefit a person, no loan, charity, or friendship: a person will have nothing except that which he sent forth from his deeds. Thus, it does not befit a person to venture into it bankrupt; so, it is mandatory upon all the Muslims to respect and honor the most valuable asset of one's wealth.

إِذَا كَانَ رَأْسُ الْمَالِ عُمْرَكَ فَاحْتَزْ

عَلَيْهِ مِنَ الْإِنْفَاقِ فِي غَيْرِ وَاجِبٍ .

'If the most valuable asset of wealth is your life, then be cautious from spending it in other than the obligations.'"[8]

Then, let the one advising himself take full advantage of the hours of his life in performing the righteous acts that he will be pleased to meet Allaah with tomorrow (in the Hereafter). Allaah says:

﴿ يَٰٓأَيُّهَا ٱلَّذِينَ ءَامَنُوا۟ ٱتَّقُوا۟ ٱللَّهَ وَلْتَنظُرْ نَفْسٌ مَّا قَدَّمَتْ لِغَدٍ وَٱتَّقُوا۟ ٱللَّهَ إِنَّ ٱللَّهَ خَبِيرٌ بِمَا تَعْمَلُونَ ۝ ﴾

"O you who believe! Fear Allaah and keep your duty to Him. So let every person look to what he has sent forth for the morrow, and fear Allaah. Verily, Allaah is All-Aware of what you do." [Soorah al-Hashr 59:18]

---

[8] Al-'Adhab an-Nameer (4/341).

THE REALITY OF RIGHTEOUS ACTIONS AND HOW, THEY CAN BE ACTUALIZED

A question arises here regarding the topic of righteous action that must be clarified, and it is: **"What is righteous action and how does the action become righteous?"**

<u>The righteous action</u>: is the deed that is beloved to Allaah (عَزَّوَجَلَّ) and his Messenger (صَلَّىٰاللَّهُعَلَيْهِوَسَلَّمَ) from the things that Allaah (سُبْحَانَهُوَتَعَالَىٰ) has instructed with as an absolute obligation or strong recommendation. And this is a wide and vast field. The righteous deeds from the hidden and apparent statements and actions are many and they are on this field of competition: a field in which the competitors compete and contenders contend from those who hope for the mercy of Allaah (سُبْحَانَهُوَتَعَالَىٰ) and success in attaining the most glorious of rewards and beautiful of resorts.

And the deed will not be righteous except with *Ikhlaas* (sincerity of the intention) for The One Who deserves

[30]

to be worshipped (جَلَّ وَعَلَا) and compliance with the way of the Messenger (صَلَّى اللَّهُ عَلَيْهِ وَسَلَّمَ). *Ikhlaas* is the foundation that righteous action is established upon; for surely, if the deeds are varying in type and numerous, but are however, not established upon *Ikhlaas* for Allaah, its doer will not benefit from them at all. Likewise, if he was to make his intention sincere, but did not follow the Messenger of Allaah (صَلَّى اللَّهُ عَلَيْهِ وَسَلَّمَ) in the way that he performed the deed, he will also not benefit from it. Thus, one will only gain benefit from deeds if they are done with *Ikhlaas* for Allaah (عَزَّوَجَلَّ) and in accordance to the way the Messenger of Allaah (صَلَّى اللَّهُ عَلَيْهِ وَسَلَّمَ). Allaah (جَلَّ جَلَالُهُ) said:

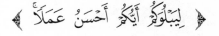

"…that He may test you which of you is best in deed." [*Soorah al-Mulk* 67:2]

The deed will not fit this description unless it is standing upon *Ikhlaas* and compliance. Fudhayl Ibn 'Iyaad (رَحِمَهُ اللَّهُ) said the meaning of "…best in deed" in this verse is:

"…its most sincere and sound." So, it was asked: 'O Aboo 'Alee, and what is 'its most sincere and sound'?'

THE REALITY OF RIGHTEOUS ACTIONS AND HOW, THEY CAN BE ACTUALIZED

He said: 'Verily, if the deed is done sincerely but is not sound and correct, it will not be accepted; and if it is sound but is not done sincerely, it will also be unaccepted, until it is both sincere and sound. So the sincere deed is that which is done solely for Allaah, and the sound one is that which conforms to the Sunnah.'" [9]

The righteous acts that Allaah (جَلَّجَلَالُهُ) loves and commanded with are many. However, what comes first and has precedence in this field are the obligations and commandments of Islaam, and this is something that must be paid attention to with regards to performing and giving care to righteous deeds. It has been reported in a Hadeeth Qudsee [10] that Allaah (سُبْحَانَهُوَتَعَالَى) says:

---

[9] Collected by Ibn Abee ad-Dunyaa in *al-Ikhlaas wan-Niyyah* (50-51) and by Aboo Nu'aym in *al-Hilyah* (8/9).
[10] **Translator's note**: It is a Hadeeth in which the Prophet (صَلَّ ٱللَّهُ عَلَيْهِ وَسَلَّمَ) narrates from Allaah.

"My slave does not get near to me with anything more beloved to me than that which I have obligated upon him." [11]

So, the obligations of Islaam and the commandments of the religion come first. If it is asked, **"What are the best and most beloved deeds?"** It will be said: **"The obligations."** An optional act should not be fulfilled before an obligation. Some people give great importance to optional acts like dutifulness, keeping ties of kinship, charity, good dealings, or anything else from the acts of worship; however, you find them neglecting great obligatory acts! Rather, you find them neglecting the biggest obligation after *Tawheed* — the Prayer. Hence, the Prayer is the pillar of the religion as has been affirmed from the Messenger of Allaah (ﷺ), he said:

مَنْ حَافَظَ عَلَيْهَا ، كَانَتْ لَهُ نُوراً وَ بُرْهَاناً وَ نَجَاةً يَوْمَ الْقِيَامَةِ ، وَ مَنْ لَمْ يُحَافِظْ عَلَيْهَا لَمْ يَكُنْ لَهُ نُورٌ وَ لَا بُرْهَانٌ وَ لَا نَجَاةٌ ، وَ يَأْتِي

11 Collected by *al-Bukhaaree* (6502) from the Hadeeth of Aboo Hurairah (رضي الله عنه).

THE REALITY OF RIGHTEOUS ACTIONS AND HOW, THEY CAN BE ACTUALIZED

يَـوْمَ الْـقِـيَـامَةِ مَـعَ قَـارُونَ وَ فِـرْعَـوْنَ وَ هَـامَـانَ وَ أُبَـيٍّ
بْـنِ خَـلَـفٍ.

"It will be for the one who safeguards it a light, a proof and salvation on the Day of Judgement; and whoever does not safeguard it, will have neither light, proof, nor salvation and he will be on the Day of Judgement with Qaaroon, Fir'awn, Haamaan and Ubay Ibn Khalaf." [12]

Therefore, when fulfilling righteous actions, the obligatory acts must be given precedence. Whoever is distracted by a mandatory act from fulfilling a supererogatory one is excused, and whoever is distracted by a supererogatory act from fulfilling a required one is deluded. How can one be preoccupied with optional deeds before the obligatory ones?! If a person was to stay up all night reading the Quraan

---

[12] Collected by Ahmad in *al-Musnad* (6576) and ad-Daaramee in his *Sunan* (2763). And Ibn Hibbaan in his *Saheeh* (1467), and adh-Dhahabee said in *Tanqeeh at-Tahqeeq* (1/300): "Its chain is good," and Ibn 'Abdil-Haadee also said in *Tanqeeh at Tahqeeq* (2/614): "The chain of this Hadeeth is good."

and, as a result, misses the *Fajr* (pre-dawn) prayer, then he is sinful for staying up as it led to the abandonment of an obligation; then how is the case for the one who stays up for sinning, disobedience and matters that displease Allaah (تَبَارَكَوَتَعَالَى) and then follows it up by sleeping and missing the Fajr prayer?! Where is the honour and due care for the righteous deeds?!

Thus, righteous actions are varying in their virtues, with the commandments of Islaam being at the forefront. After the obligations, if it is asked: **"Which deed is better?"** It will be said as mentioned by Shaykhul-Islaam (Ibn Taymiyyah) and other than him from the people of knowledge: There is no detailed answer regarding that, except that it is according to a person's case, place and current time. Though, an encompassing statement can be made regarding this topic, and it is:

"The best and most virtuous deed at any given time is that which is most compliant with the Sunnah at that specific time."

This is a precious principle regarding the superiority of deeds over each other in virtue and determining which of them is better.

THE SUPERIORITY OF THE PEOPLE OF *EEMAAN* OVER EACH OTHER IN RIGHTEOUS DEEDS

If the deeds themselves are differing in virtue over one another, then certainly the people of *Eemaan* themselves are superior over one another in the performance of those good deeds. They are not all on the same level; rather, between them are vast differences and stark contrasts. Allaah (عَزَّوَجَلَّ) said:

$$﴿ ثُمَّ أَوْرَثْنَا الْكِتَابَ الَّذِينَ اصْطَفَيْنَا مِنْ عِبَادِنَا$$

$$فَمِنْهُمْ ظَالِمٌ لِنَفْسِهِ وَمِنْهُم مُّقْتَصِدٌ وَمِنْهُمْ سَابِقٌ$$

$$بِالْخَيْرَاتِ بِإِذْنِ اللَّهِ ذَلِكَ هُوَ الْفَضْلُ الْكَبِيرُ ۝$$

$$جَنَّاتُ عَدْنٍ يَدْخُلُونَهَا ﴾$$

"Then We gave the (Book the Quraan) as an inheritance to such of Our slaves whom We

chose (the followers of Muhammad (صَلَّىٰاللَّهُ عَلَيْهِ وَسَلَّمَ)). Then of them are some who wrong their selves, and of them are some who follow a middle course, and of them are some who are, by Allaah's Leave, foremost in good deeds. That (inheritance of the Quraan), which is indeed a great grace. (33) 'Adn (Eden) Paradise (everlasting Gardens) will they enter." [*Soorah al-Faatir* 35:32-33]

Ibn al-Qayyim (رَحِمَهُ ٱللَّهُ) said:

> "They (the aforementioned in the verse) are all ready for the journey and are certain about their return to Allaah; however, they are varying in their provisions, the way they store and select it, as well as the manner of the their movement, its speed and slowness. As for **"the one who wrongs himself,"** then he is short in provisions and does not take that which will make him reach his abode both in its proper quantity and quality. He is negligent in supplying himself with the desired provision, and instead equips himself with what will harm him in his path—a harm whose end result he will find when he reaches the abode with what he provisioned himself from it.

[37]

"The one who follows a middle course," on the other hand, limits himself to the provision that will make him reach his goal and does not engage himself in the goods of the profitable trades, nor does he equip himself with that which will harm him. So, he is safe and productive, but has, however, missed out on the profitable trade and its varying types of superior gains.

As for **"the one foremost in good deeds,"** his concern is in obtaining profits and capitalizing on the gains of the trades since he knows the current, lucrative profit's worth. Thus, he considers anything that he saves from whatever is in his hands and does not use in trade to be a loss and as a result finds his gains on a day when the merchants will be joyful with their earnings. He is like a man who knows that in front of him is a land of wealth in which one can earn ten to seven hundred or even more rewards and he has a storehouse and expertise in getting around that land as well as expertise in business. If he were able to sell his clothes and all his belongings in order

[38]

to prepare for business in that land, he would do it. And similar to this is the case of the one who is foremost in good deeds by Allaah's leave; he considers any time used in other than trade (performance of righteous acts) to be a clear loss."[13]

The one who wrongs himself was mentioned first in this verse so that he does not despair and lose hope and the one who is foremost in fulfilling good deeds is mentioned last so he does not become afflicted with self-amazement; and his lead in the performance of good is a favor from Allaah upon him: **"by Allaah's Leave"** and Allaah (جَلَّجَلَالُه) is the Bestower of Favour and the Granter of Bounties. He says:

$$ \text{﴿ وَلَوْلَا فَضْلُ ٱللَّهِ عَلَيْكُمْ وَرَحْمَتُهُ مَا زَكَىٰ مِنكُم مِّنْ أَحَدٍ أَبَدًا وَلَـٰكِنَّ ٱللَّهَ يُزَكِّى مَن يَشَآءُ ﴾} $$

"And had it not been for the Grace of Allaah and His Mercy on you, not one of you would ever have been pure from sins. However, Allaah purifies (guides to Islaam) whom He wills." [*Soorah an-Noor* 24:21]

---

[13] *Tareeq al-Hijratayn* by Ibn al-Qayyim (pg. 404-405)

THE SUPERIORITY OF THE PEOPLE OF EEMAAN OVER EACH OTHER IN RIGHTEOUS DEEDS

Hence, from the things that we should understand from this topic is that the slave is unable to perform anything from the righteous actions and purifying acts of obedience unless Allaah (عَزَّوَجَلَّ) aids him in it and makes it easy for him. The Prophet (صَلَّى اللَّهُ عَلَيْهِ وَسَلَّمَ) said to Mu'aadh Ibn Jabal (رَضِيَ اللَّهُ عَنْهُ):

يَا مُعَاذُ، إِنِّي لَأُحِبُّكَ ، فَقَالَ لَهُ مُعَاذٌ : ((بِأَبِي وَ أُمِّي يَا رَسُولَ الله وَ أَنَا أُحِبُّكَ))، فَقَالَ : ((أُوصِيكَ يَا مُعَاذُ لَا تَدَعَنَّ فِي دُبُرِ كُلِّ صَلَاةٍ أَنْ تَقُولَ : اللَّهُمَّ أَعِنِّي عَلَى ذِكْرِكَ وَ شُكْرِكَ وَ حُسْنِ عِبَادَتِكَ)) .

"O Mu'aadh, verily I love you!' Mu'aadh replied to him, saying: 'May my mother and father be ransomed for you O Messenger of Allaah, and I love you.' Then he (the Messenger) said: 'I advise you O Mu'aadh, to never forget to say at the end of every Prayer:

'Allaahumma a'inni 'ala dhikrika wa shukrika wa husni 'ibaadatika'

(O Allaah, help me to remember You, give thanks to You and worship You in the best manner)." [14]

Regarding righteous acts, it is befitting that the Muslim observes certain matters: he should distance himself from matters that will cause weariness and boredom with the acts of worship and eventually complete abandonment—as has happened to many people. It has been reported in the *Saheeh* that the Messenger of Allaah (ﷺ) was asked:

أَيُّ الْعَمَلِ أَحَبُّ إِلَى الله ؟ قَالَ : ((أَدْوَمُهُ وَ إِنْ قَلَّ))

"Which of the deeds is most beloved to Allaah? He said: 'The most consistent and regular of them even if it is a little.'" [15]

---

[14] Collected by Aboo Daawood (1522), Ahmad (22119, 22126), and authenticated by al-Albaanee *in Saheeh Sunan Abee Daawood* (1362)

[15] Collected by *Muslim* (782) from the Hadeeth of *Ummul-Mu'mineen* 'Aa'ishah (رضي الله عنها).

THE SUPERIORITY OF THE PEOPLE OF EEMAAN OVER EACH OTHER IN RIGHTEOUS DEEDS

For example, your praying two units of Prayer every night is greater and better for you than praying several times in one night, or three or four or even five nights and then leaving that Prayer. And *Ummul-Mu'mineen* 'Aa'ishah (رَضِيَاللَّهُعَنْهَا) said:

دَخَلَ عَلَيَّ رَسُولُ الله ، وَ عِنْدِي اِمْرَأَةٌ ، فَقَالَ : ((مَنْ هَذِهِ ؟)) ، فَقُلْتُ : ((اِمْرَأَةٌ لَا تَنَامُ تُصَلِّي)) ، قَالَ : ((عَلَيْكُمْ مِنَ الْعَمَلِ مَا تُطِيقُونَ، فَوَ الله لَا يَمَلُّ اللهُ حَتَّى تَمَلُّوا)) . وَ كَانَ أَحَبُّ الدِّينِ إِلَيْهِ مَا دَاوَمَ عَلَيْهِ صَاحِبُهُ .

"The Messenger of Allaah entered upon me while there was a woman with me and asked: 'Who is she?' I replied: 'She is a woman who does not sleep and prays [all night].' He said: 'What is upon you from the deeds is that which you can bear, by Allaah, He will not be bored until you become bored,' and the most beloved

religious deed to him was the one that its doer
continuously performed.'" [16]

So, let the servant perform from the deeds and the
optional acts that which he can bear. However, he
must compel himself to fulfill the obligations since he
will be punished if he leaves them. As for the optional
acts, then let him perform from them that which he
can do consistently even if it is a little; as the most
beloved deed to Allaah (سُبْحَانَهُوَتَعَالَى) is the most
consistent and regular even if it is small. An-
Nawawee (رَحِمَهُ ٱللَّهُ) said:

"In it (the Hadeeth) is an encouragement to
stay constant in performing deeds and that its
small bit that is regular is better than
numerous ones that are inconsistent. And this
is the case because consistency with the little
bit leads to consistency with obedience to
Allaah, Dhikr (words of remembrance),
observance (of Allaah's rights), having an
intention and sincerity, as well as devoutness
to The Creator (سُبْحَانَهُوَتَعَالَى). Also, the small,
consistent amount of deeds will bear fruit that

---

[16] Collected by *al-Bukhaaree* (43), *Muslim* (785)

THE SUPERIORITY OF THE PEOPLE OF
EEMAAN OVER EACH OTHER IN
RIGHTEOUS DEEDS

is several times more than the high number of inconsistent deeds."

With regards to Prayer, the consistent number that a Muslim should observe every night and day is forty *Raka'aat* (units of prayer) as explained by Ibn al-Qayyim (رَحِمَهُٱللَّه) when he mentioned the Prophet's (صَلَّىٱللَّهُعَلَيْهِوَسَلَّم) consistent number of prayers that he offered:

"The total of his constant portion in the day and night is forty Raka'aat that he would always observe: seventeen mandatory ones (for the five daily prayers), ten or twelve that are *Rawaatib*[17], and eleven or thirteen that he stood up at night to pray; which sums up to forty *Raka'aat*...Thus, it is befitting that the slave persists in always offering this specified amount until death. And what a swift answer and opening of the door it will be for the one who knocks on it forty times every day and night."

---

[17]**Translator's note**: The *Rawaatib* are the two optional units offered before *Fajr*, two or four before *Dhuhr*, two after *Dhuhr*, two after *Maghrib* and two after *'Ishaa'*.

PROFITABLE TRADES

Therefore, it behooves every Muslim to cling to this daily specified amount and not decrease anything from it, and if he does more, then this is an increase in goodness.

If Allaah expands a servant's life, he should remember that the best of the people is the one who lives a long life and has good actions. At-Tirmidhi and Ahmad report that a Bedouin asked:

يَا رَسُولَ اللهِ مَنْ خَيْرُ النَّاسِ ، قَالَ : ((مَنْ طَالَ عُمُرُهُ وَ حَسُنَ عَمَلُهُ)) .

"O Messenger of Allaah! Who is the best of the people? He said: 'He whose life is long and his deeds are good.'" [18]

He should also remember the statement of the Prophet (عَلَيْهِ ٱلصَّلَاةُ وَٱلسَّلَامُ):

إِنَّمَا الْأَعْمَالُ بِالْخَوَاتِيمِ

---

[18] Collected by at-Tirmidhi (2329, 2330), and Ahmad (17680, 20415) and authenticated by at-Tirmidhi and al-Albaanee in *Saheeh al-Jaami'* (3296, 3297)

[45]

THE SUPERIORITY OF THE PEOPLE OF EEMAAN OVER EACH OTHER IN RIGHTEOUS DEEDS

"Surely, the deeds are determined by the final actions."

He says in another narration:

وَ إِنَّمَا الْأَعْمَالُ بِخَوَاتِيمِهَا .

"Surely, the deeds are determined by their end." [19]

Thus, one should strive in increasing his performance of acts of obedience, righteous deeds, and devotion to Allaah (سُبْحَانَهُ وَتَعَالَى).

"Sulaymaan Ibn 'Abdul-Malik once entered the Masjid and noticed an old man. He called for him, saying:

> 'O Shaykh! Do you love death?' He said: 'No.' Then, he asked: 'Why?' He said: 'Youth is gone along with its evil and old age has come with its good. When I stand, I say, *'Bismillaah'* (In The name of Allaah) and when I sit, I say, *'Al-Hamdu lillaah'* (all praise and thanks are due

---

[19] Collected by *al-Bukhaaree* (6493,6607) from the *Hadeeth* of *Sahl Ibn Sa'ad as-Saa'idee* (رَضِيَ اللَّهُ عَنْهُ)

to Allaah); so, I love that this remains for me.'"
20

If he use to transgress against himself and was negligent, then let him rectify himself—what is he expecting from his transgression and negligence?!

Fudhayl Ibn 'Iyaadh said to a man:

قَالَ الْفُضَيْلُ بْنُ عِيَاضٍ لِرَجُلٍ : ((كَمْ أَتَتْ عَلَيْكَ ؟ ، قَالَ : سِتُّونَ سِنَةً ، قَالَ : فَأَنْتَ مُنْذُ سِتِّينَ سِنَةً تَسِيرُ إِلَى رَبِّكَ تُوشِكُ أَنْ تَبْلُغَ ، فَقَالَ الرَّجُلُ : يَا أَبَا عَلِيٍّ : إِنَّا لله وَ إِنَّا إِلَيْهِ رَاجِعُونَ ، قَالَ لَهُ الْفُضَيْلُ : تَعْلَمُ مَا تَقُولُ ؟ ، قَالَ الرَّجُلُ : قُلْتُ : إِنَّا لله وَإِنَّا إِلَيْهِ رَاجِعُونَ، قَالَ الْفُضَيْلُ : تَعْلَمُ مَا تَفْسِيرُهُ ؟ قَالَ الرَّجُلُ : فَسِّرْهُ لَنَا يَا أَبَا عَلِيٍّ ، قَالَ : قَوْلُكَ : إِنَّا لله ، تَقُولُ : أَنَا لله عَبْدٌ ، وَ أَنَا إِلَى الله رَاجِعٌ ، فَمَنْ

---

[47]

THE SUPERIORITY OF THE PEOPLE OF EEMAAN OVER EACH OTHER IN RIGHTEOUS DEEDS

عَلِمَ أَنَّهُ عَبْدُ الله وَ أَنَّهُ إِلَيْهِ رَاجِعٌ، فَلْيَعْلَمْ بِأَنَّهُ مَوْقُوفٌ، وَ مَنْ عَلِمَ بِأَنَّهُ مَوْقُوفٌ، فَلْيَعْلَمْ بِأَنَّهُ مَسْؤُولٌ، وَ مَنْ عَلِمَ أَنَّهث مَسْؤُولٌ، فَلْيُعِدَّ لِلسُّؤَالِ جَوَاباً، فَقَالَ الرَّجُلُ : فَمَا الْحِيلَةُ؟ قَالَ : يَسِيرَةٌ، قَالَ : مَا هِيَ؟ قَالَ : تُحْسِنُ فِيمَا بَقِيَ يُغْفَرُ لَكَ مَا مَضَى وَ مَا بَقِيَ ؛ فَإِنَّكَ إِنْ أَسَأْتَ فِيمَا بَقِيَ أُخِذْتَ بِمَا مَضَى وَ مَا بَقِيَ))

"How old are you?" He said: **"Sixty years."** He said to the man: **"So since sixty years you have been making the journey to your Lord and are nearing death."** The man said: **"O Aboo 'Abdillaah *'Innaa Lillaahi wa Innaa Ilayhi Raaji'oon'* (to Allaah we belong and to Him we will return)."** Fudhayl said to him: **"Do you know what you are saying?"** He replied: **"I said, 'to Allaah we belong and to him we shall return.'"**

Fudhayl said:

"Do you know its explanation?"

The man said:

"Explain it to us O Aboo 'Abdillaah."

He said:

"Your statement 'to Allaah we belong," means, "I am a slave to Allaah and will return to Him." Therefore, whoever knows that he is Allaah's slave and will return to him, should realize that he is a prisoner. And whoever realizes that he is a prisoner, should know that he will be questioned and whoever knows that he will be questioned, should prepare an answer for the interrogation."

The man said: "So what is the solution?" He said: "It is easy." The man said: "What is it?" He said: "Rectify that which remains [from your life] and you will be forgiven for that which has passed and that which remains. For verily, if you are evil in that which remains, you will be held accountable for what has passed and what's left." [21]

---

[21] Collected by Aboo Nu'aym in *al-Hilyah* (8/113)

THE SUPERIORITY OF THE PEOPLE OF EEMAAN OVER EACH OTHER IN RIGHTEOUS DEEDS

Thus, this is from the things that clarify the statement of the Prophet (ﷺ):

وَ إِنَّمَا الْأَعْمَالُ بِالْخَوَاتِيمِ .

"Surely, actions are determined by their end."

Then, if the slave is given success to perform certain deeds—whether they are small in number or high—he should not become conceited by them even if they are numerous. He should remember the state of the believers that Allaah has mentioned in *Soorah al-Mu'minoon*:

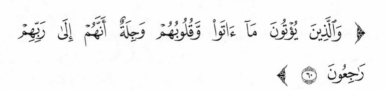

"And those who give that (their charity) which they give (and also do other good deeds) with their hearts full of fear (whether their alms and charities, have been accepted or not), because they are sure to return to their Lord (for reckoning)." [*Soorah al-Mu'minoon* 23:60]

Ummul-Mu'mineen 'Aa'ishah (رَضِيَاللَّهُعَنْهَا) asked the Prophet (صَلَّىاللَّهُعَلَيْهِوَسَلَّمَ) about this verse, she said:

﴿ وَالَّذِينَ يُؤْتُونَ مَا ءَاتَوا وَّقُلُوبُهُمْ وَجِلَةٌ أَنَّهُمْ إِلَىٰ رَبِّهِمْ رَاجِعُونَ ۝ ﴾ قُلْتُ : ((يَا رَسُولَ الله ! أَ هُوَ الرَّجُلُ الَّذِي يَزْنِي وَ يَسْرِقُ وَ يَشْرَبُ الْخَمْرَ)) قَالَ : ((لَا يَا بِنْتَ أَبِي بَكْرٍ - أَوْ يَا بِنْتَ الصِّدِّيقِ - وَ لَكِنَّهُ الرَّجُلُ يَصُومُ وَ يَتَصَدَّقُ وَ يُصَلِّي وَ هُوَ يَخَافُ أَنْ لَا يُقْبَلَ مِنْهُ)).

"I said: 'O Messenger of Allah,

{And those who give that (their charity) which they give (and also do other good deeds) with their hearts full of fear.} [*Soorah al-Mu'minoon* 23:60]

Is this the one who commits adultery, steals and drinks alcohol?' He said: 'No, O daughter of Aboo Bakr' – or he said, 'No, O daughter of Siddeeq' – rather it is a man who fasts, gives

THE SUPERIORITY OF THE PEOPLE OF EEMAAN OVER EACH OTHER IN RIGHTEOUS DEEDS

charity and prays, but fears that they will not be accepted from him.'" [22]

Thus, it has authentically come in a Hadeeth that our Prophet (صَلَّىٰاللَّهُعَلَيْهِوَسَلَّمَ) said:

((لَنْ يُدْخِلَ أَحَداً مِنْكُمْ عَمَلُهُ الْجَنَّةَ)) قَالُوا : وَ لَا أَنْتَ ؟ يَا رَسُولَ الله قَالَ : ((وَ لَا أَنَا ، إِلَّا أَنْ يَتَغَمَّدَنِي اللهُ مِنْهُ بِفَضْلٍ وَ رَحْمَةٍ)) .

"'None of you enters Paradise due to his deeds.' They said: 'Not even you O Messenger of Allaah?' He said: 'Not even me unless Allaah envelops me with His favor and mercy.'" [23]

Hence, the Muslim must not become arrogant, but instead should increase in righteous deeds and ask Allaah (تَبَارَكَوَتَعَالَى) for acceptance, His pleasure and *Tawfeeq*. Also, regarding this topic of righteous deeds,

---

[22] Collected by Ahmad (25705), and at-Tirmidhi (3170) and Ibn Maajah (4198), authenticated by al-Albaanee in *as-Saheehah* (162)
[23] Collected by *al-Bukhaaree* (5673), and *Muslim* (2816) from the Hadeeth of Aboo Hurairah (رَضِيَاللَّهُعَنْهُ)

the wise believer should be aware of the servant's second life after his death. This is an aspect of deeds that only those granted success from Allaah's servants can comprehend: so one of them would have another life for deeds after death, and this is the second life. Regarding this, he (ﷺ) said:

إِذَا مَاتَ الْإِنْسَانُ انْقَطَعَ عَنْهُ عَمَلُهُ إِلَّا مِنْ ثَلَاثَةٍ مِنْ صَدَقَةٍ جَارِيَةٍ أَوْ عِلْمٍ يُنْتَفَعُ بِهِ أَوْ وَلَدٍ صَالِحٍ يَدْعُو لَهُ.

"When a person dies, all his deeds will cease except from three: ongoing charity, or knowledge that others benefit from, or a righteous child that supplicates for him." [24]

He said in another Hadeeth:

سَبْعٌ يَجْرِي لِلْعَبْدِ أَجْرُهُنَّ مِنْ بَعْدِ مَوْتِهِ وَ هُوَ فِي قَبْرِهِ: مَنْ عَلَّمَ عِلْماً ، أَوْ كَرَى نَهَراً ، أَوْ حَفَرَ بِئْراً ، أَوْ غَرَسَ نَخْلاً ، أَوْ بَنَى مَسْجِداً ،

---

[24] Collected by *Muslim* (1631) from the Hadeeth of Aboo Hurairah (رضي الله عنه)

THE SUPERIORITY OF THE PEOPLE OF EEMAAN OVER EACH OTHER IN RIGHTEOUS DEEDS

أَوْ وَرَّثَ مُصْحَفاً ، أَوْ تَرَكَ وَلَداً يَسْتَغْفِرُ لَهُ بَعْدَ مَوْتِهِ .

"The reward for seven things will continue to accumulate for the servant even after his death when he is in his grave: knowledge that he taught, a stream that he dug, a well that he drilled, a date palm that he planted, a Masjid that he built, a *Mushaf* (the Noble Quraan) that he donated, or a child that he left behind who seeks forgiveness for him after his death." [25]

This is astonishing: some of those deceased in their graves will continue to have rewards accumulating for them every day and night — their rewards multiplying — while others walk on the earth as days, nights and months go by without attaining any reward, but actually committing sins and misdeeds — refuge is sought with Allaah! Yaa Subhaanallaah! What a great difference! Where are the consideration

---

[25] Collected by al-Bazzaar in his *Musnad* (7289), and Aboo Nu'aym in *al-Hilyah* (2/343) from the Hadeeth of Anas Ibn Maalik (رَضِيَاللَّهُعَنْهُ), authenticated by al-Albaanee in *Saheeh al-Jaami'* (3602)

and the learning of a lesson?! Where is the remembrance?!

This is a matter which a person should strive against his soul to learn and deeply understand and then strive against it in the performance of deeds so that he will not be remorseful one day when remorse will be of no benefit. Whoever is heedless and neglectful will surely be in deep regret in many instances where his regret will be of no avail to him. Thus, there are many verses in the Noble Quraan that highlight the unfathomable regret there will be over the disregard given to *Eemaan* and righteous actions; whether it is at the time of death as mentioned by Allaah (سُبْحَانَهُوَتَعَالَ):

﴿ حَتَّىٰٓ إِذَا جَآءَ أَحَدَهُمُ ٱلۡمَوۡتُ قَالَ رَبِّ ٱرۡجِعُونِ ۝ لَعَلِّيٓ أَعۡمَلُ صَٰلِحٗا فِيمَا تَرَكۡتُۚ كَلَّآۚ إِنَّهَا كَلِمَةٌ هُوَ قَآئِلُهَاۖ وَمِن وَرَآئِهِم بَرۡزَخٌ إِلَىٰ يَوۡمِ يُبۡعَثُونَ ۝ ﴾

"Until, when death comes to one of them (those who join partners with Allaah), he says:

[55]

THE SUPERIORITY OF THE PEOPLE OF EEMAAN OVER EACH OTHER IN RIGHTEOUS DEEDS

"My Lord! Send me back, (99) "So that I may do good in that which I have left behind!" No! It is but a word that he speaks, and behind them is *Barzakh* (a barrier) until the Day when they will be resurrected." [*Soorah al-Mu'minoon* 23:99-100]

Or on the Day of Judgement:

﴿ وَأَنذِرِ ٱلنَّاسَ يَوْمَ يَأْتِيهِمُ ٱلْعَذَابُ فَيَقُولُ ٱلَّذِينَ ظَلَمُوا۟ رَبَّنَآ أَخِّرْنَآ إِلَىٰٓ أَجَلٍ قَرِيبٍ نُّجِبْ دَعْوَتَكَ وَنَتَّبِعِ ٱلرُّسُلَ أَوَلَمْ تَكُونُوٓا۟ أَقْسَمْتُم مِّن قَبْلُ مَا لَكُم مِّن زَوَالٍ ﴿٤٤﴾ ﴾

"And warn (O Muhammad (ﷺ)) mankind of the Day when the torment will come unto them; then the wrong-doers will say: "Our Lord! Respite us for a little while, we will answer Your Call and follow the Messengers!" (It will be said): "Had you not sworn aforetime that you would not leave (the world for the Hereafter)." [*Soorah Ibrahim* 14:44]

Or when standing in front of The Exalted and All Mighty Compeller (i.e., Allaah (سُبْحَانَهُ وَتَعَالَى)):

$$﴿ وَلَوْ تَرَىٰ إِذِ ٱلْمُجْرِمُونَ نَاكِسُواْ رُءُوسِهِمْ عِندَ رَبِّهِمْ رَبَّنَآ أَبْصَرْنَا وَسَمِعْنَا فَٱرْجِعْنَا نَعْمَلْ صَٰلِحًا إِنَّا مُوقِنُونَ ١٢ ﴾$$

"And if you only could see when the Mujrimoon (criminals, disbelievers, polytheists, sinners, etc.) shall hang their heads before their Lord (saying): "Our Lord! We have now seen and heard, so send us back (to the world), that we will do righteous good deeds. Verily! We now believe with certainty." [*Soorah as-Sajdah* 32:12]

Or in the Hell-Fire when he is entered into it, he will be tremendously remorseful; Allaah (عَزَّوَجَلَّ) says regarding the disbelievers:

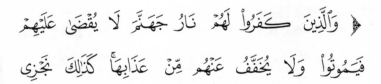

$$﴿ وَٱلَّذِينَ كَفَرُواْ لَهُمْ نَارُ جَهَنَّمَ لَا يُقْضَىٰ عَلَيْهِمْ فَيَمُوتُواْ وَلَا يُخَفَّفُ عَنْهُم مِّنْ عَذَابِهَا كَذَٰلِكَ نَجْزِى$$

THE SUPERIORITY OF THE PEOPLE OF EEMAAN OVER EACH OTHER IN RIGHTEOUS DEEDS

كُلَّ كَفُورٍ ۝ وَهُمْ يَصْطَرِخُونَ فِيهَا رَبَّنَآ أَخْرِجْنَا نَعْمَلْ صَلِحًا غَيْرَ ٱلَّذِى كُنَّا نَعْمَلُ أَوَلَمْ نُعَمِّرْكُم مَّا يَتَذَكَّرُ فِيهِ مَن تَذَكَّرَ وَجَآءَكُمُ ٱلنَّذِيرُ فَذُوقُواْ فَمَا لِلظَّلِمِينَ مِن نَّصِيرٍ ۝

"But those who disbelieve, (in the Oneness of Allaah - Islaamic Monotheism) for them will be the Fire of Hell. Neither will it have a complete killing effect on them so that they die nor shall its torment be lightened for them. Thus do We requite every disbeliever! (36) Within they will cry: "Our Lord! Bring us out, we shall do righteous good deeds, not (the evil deeds) that we used to do." (Allaah will reply): "Did We not give you lives long enough, so that whosoever would receive admonition, could receive it? So the warner came to you. So taste you (the evil of your deeds). For the Zâlimoon (polytheists and wrongdoers) there is no helper." [*Soorah al-Faatir* 35:36-37]

These are instances in which there will be this regret
that will, however, be of no benefit. Thus, the
intelligent one will take a lesson from this — since he is
still in the abode for actions — and rectify his state and
deeds and hold himself to account before Allaah
(سُبْحَانَهُوَتَعَالَى) does so. There comes in a Hadeeth Qudsee:

يَا عِبَادِي : إِنَّمَا هِيَ أَعْمَالُكُمْ أُحْصِيهَا لَكُمْ
، ثُمَّ أُوَفِّيـكُمْ إِيَّاهَا ، فَمَنْ وَجَدَ خَيْراً فَلْيَحْمَدِ
اللهَ ، وَ مَنْ وَجَدَ غَيْرَ ذَلِكَ فَلَا يَلُـومَنَّ إِلَّا نَفْسَهُ .

**"O My servants, it is but your deeds that I
reckon up for you and then recompense you
for, so let him who finds good, praise and
thank Allaah, and let him who finds other than
that, blame no one but himself."** [26]

One of the pious predecessors wanted to admonish a
man, so he took him to the cemetery. When they
stopped near the graves, he asked him:

---

[26] Collected by *Muslim* (2577) from the Hadeeth of Aboo Dhar al-
Ghifaaree (رَضِيَاللَهُعَنْهُ)

THE SUPERIORITY OF THE PEOPLE OF EEMAAN OVER EACH OTHER IN RIGHTEOUS DEEDS

لَوْ كُنْتَ مَكَانَ هَؤُلَاءِ مَاذَا تَتَمَنَّى ؟ قَالَ :
أَتَمَنَّى أَنْ يُعِيدَنِي اللهُ لِلْحَيَاةِ الدُّنْيَا لِأَعْمَلَ
صَالِحاً غَيْرَ الَّذِي أَعْمَلُهُ ، فَقَالَ لَهُ : أَنْتَ الْآنَ
فِيمَا تَتَمَنَّاهُ .

"If you were in their place, what would you wish for?"

He said:

"I would wish that Allaah return me back to the Worldly life so that I could perform righteous actions and not what I am upon now."

He said to him:

"You are now in what you would wish for."

Meaning, you are now in the abode for actions; the intelligent one will hold himself to account before Allaah (عَزَّوَجَلَّ) does and he will weigh his deeds before they are weighed on the meeting day with Allaah (سُبْحَانَهُ وَتَعَالَى).

[60]

So, the servant must be aware of sins, for verily,

الـذُّنُوبُ تُنْسِي الْعَبْدَ حَظَّهُ مِنْ هَذِهِ التِّجَارَةِ الرَّابِحَةِ ، وَ تُشْغِلُهُ بِالتِّجَارَةِ الْخَاسِرَةِ ، وَ كَفَى بِذَلِكَ عُقُوبَةً .

"Sins make the servant forget his share from this profitable trade and busy him with the losing trade, and that is sufficient as a punishment." [27]

May Allaah grant us safety and protection.

In conclusion, these are some modest references regarding this topic — and it is a vast and massive one. I ask Allaah (جَلَّ وَعَلَا) with His beautiful names and lofty attributes to grant us all *Tawfeeq* in that which is beloved and pleasing to Him from the righteous statements and actions, that He beautifies us with the beauty of *Eemaan*, and that He make us those who are guided and a cause for guidance to others, and not those who are misguided and a reason for misguidance to others.

---

[27] *al-Jawaab al-Kaafee* by Ibn al-Qayyim (pg. 248)

THE SUPERIORITY OF THE PEOPLE OF EEMAAN OVER EACH OTHER IN RIGHTEOUS DEEDS

And may He raise the rank of His slave and Messenger, our Prophet Muhammad, his family and companions and grant them all peace.

Made in the USA
Middletown, DE
08 November 2024

63682772R00038